OUR TINY SERVANTS

Molds and Yeasts

OUR TINY SERVANTS

Molds and Yeasts

Written by

BERNICE KOHN

Illustrated by

JOHN KAUFMANN

Prentice-Hall, Inc.
Englewood Cliffs
New Jersey

For Bonnie, Judy and Gene

Fourth printing. . . . . December, 1966

Library of Congress Catalog Card Number: 62-8715

Printed in the United States of America

64442-T

CONTENTS

Chapter I

TINY PLANTS

Have you ever left a wet towel in the bottom of the clothes hamper? Or put a damp pair of sneakers away in your closet? If you have, they were probably covered with nasty little black spots the next time you looked. And if you showed them to your mother she may have told you that the spots were called *mildew*.

Did you ever look for an orange to eat and find one all the way in the back of the refrigerator? Perhaps it had been there for a long time and was covered with soft, greenish-blue fuzz.

Or have you ever found a piece of stale bread which had grown black "whiskers?"

7

Well, the mildew spots on the sneakers, the fuzz on the orange, and the whiskers on the bread are related to each other. They are all *molds*.

Molds are really tiny plants. They are so very tiny that we can't see them unless there are many of them growing together. It might take fifty or sixty of them to make a row as thick as one of your hairs.

If we want to look at just one mold plant we have to use a microscope to make it large enough to see. Men haven't always had microscopes with which to see such small things—and so for a long time they just didn't see them.

The first crude microscope was probably made about the year 1590 by a Dutch maker of eyeglasses named Zacharias Janssen. Some people think the astronomer, Galileo, invented the microscope. We aren't really sure.

But we *do* know who made the first important discoveries about the tiny plants and animals that can be seen under a microscope. These tiny living things are called *microbes* (say: *MY-krobes*). The word microbe comes from two Greek words—*Mikros-small,* and *Bios-life.* Microbes were first studied by a Dutchman named Leeuwenhoek (say: *Lee-U-wen-hoke*) who made his own microscopes. Far from being an educated scientist, this man was the owner of a dry goods store. In his spare time, he was the janitor of the city hall in Delft, Holland.

ANTONY VAN LEEUWENHOEK
1632 - 1723

Leeuwenhoek was a curious man. He enjoyed looking at things through a microscope so that he could see them better. But he wanted to see still more. He began to see things that no one had ever seen before. When he found that there were no stronger lenses than the ones he had, he began to grind his own. During his lifetime Leeuwenhoek made 247 microscopes. Some of them could magnify 270 times—enough to make a grain of rice look like a football! It was probably this curious janitor who first looked at a bit of mold and saw a garden full of beautiful plants.

There are many kinds of molds and they all have long scientific names which tell something about them. One

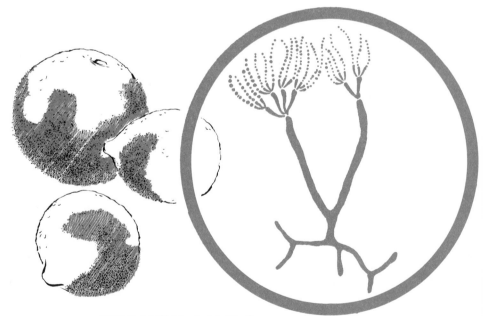

PENICILLIUM

of the most interesting is the mold that can turn an orange or a lemon into a blue-green fuzz ball. It is called *Penicillium* (say: *Pen-i-SILL-ee-um*). When the early scientists saw this mold under the microscope it seemed to have a small brush at the tip. They named it for the Latin word *penicillus* (say: *pen-i-SILL-us*)—a paint brush. The earliest writing was done with a brush and our modern writing tool, a pencil, gets its name from the same word.

All molds are food-robbers. They steal their food from other plants because they cannot make their own.

All of the ordinary plants that you know use sunlight to make food in their leaves. The green coloring matter acts as a kind of food factory.

Do you wonder why molds can't make food too? Well, it's because they are never green. They have no food factories so they take the food they need from green plants.

The scientific name for food-robbing plants is *fungi* (say: *FUN-jee*). One such plant is called a *fungus* (say: *FUN-gus*).

Fungi are never found all alone. They always grow *on* something. Bread mold feeds on bread. Can you guess what feeds the mildew on your sneakers? Well, sneakers are made of cotton and the cotton was once a growing green plant. Even though a cotton sneaker doesn't *look*

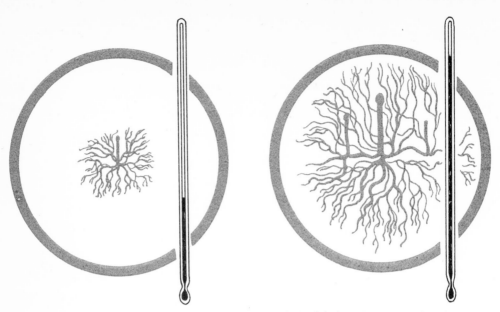

MOLDS GROW FAST WHEN IT IS WARM

anything like a plant, it still has enough plant food left to feed the mold. Molds often grow on damp wood or soggy paper. Remember that wood was once a tree, and paper is made from wood.

Molds can grow in both hot and cold places but they grow much faster when it is warm. The colder it gets the more slowly molds grow. That is why foods get moldy more quickly in the summer time than in the winter, and why we put foods into a refrigerator to keep them from spoiling.

The refrigerator keeps food very well for a few days. But if we want to keep food for a long time we put it into the deep-freeze instead because it is much colder.

Some years ago a group of explorers in northern Siberia found the frozen bodies of *mammoths*. These extinct woolly elephants had been buried in the ice for thousands of years. When the explorers thawed the meat they found it to be so fresh that they fed it to their sled dogs!

Chapter II

MAGIC
SEEDS

If you decided to start a flower garden, you would probably go to the store and buy some seeds. Then you would plant them in the ground. But if you want to start a mold garden you don't have to do nearly so much.

As a matter of fact, you don't have to do *anything* except get a good growing-place ready. The seeds will come by magic and will even plant themselves!

Did you say that magic is only for fairy stories? You are quite right—so let's take a close look at some molds under the microscope and see where these seeds *really* come from.

The first thing we notice is a big batch of threads that grow in all directions. They look a little bit like a tangled spider web.

If we can pick out one single thread and examine it carefully we see that it has branches like a Christmas tree. Each branch has a whole series of new branches. At the ends of some of these we see little round balls. They are really hollow cases and each one is chock-full of very tiny seeds called *spores*. The spores are the mold plant's seeds.

The threads and their cases are all colorless, but as we look we get a surprise. One of the spore cases has become ripe and it suddenly bursts open like a silent firecracker. We see hundreds of beautifully colored spores.

Now we have learned something: mold plants have no color at all. It is only their spores which make them look black or blue or pink or almost any other color.

A single spore is so small that perhaps a thousand of them would fit on the head of a pin. It is so light that it is lighter than the lightest thing you can think of. It is much, much lighter than milkweed fluff. It is lighter

MOLDS AS SEEN THROUGH A MICROSCOPE

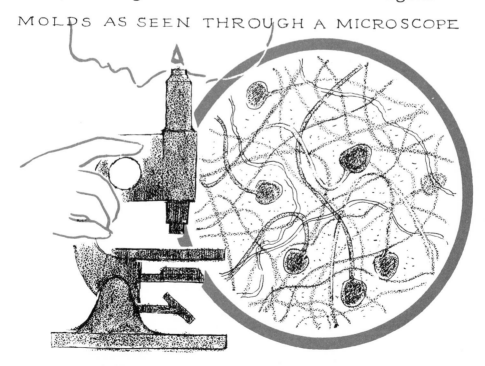

than the grains of dust you see in a beam of sunshine. It is so light that it can just hang in the air or float about for days and not fall down.

The tiniest breath of air, even the breeze you make when you walk through a room will make the spores dance. The storm you make when you sneeze or turn on the electric fan will send them scurrying far and wide.

Each mold growth may produce millions and millions of spores and they all float around looking for a place to grow. They are in the air all around you right now, and on the floor and on your shoes and even on your hair!

Unlike green plants, molds do not need any light but they do need air, food, and *water*. The mildew could never have grown on your towel if you had hung it up to dry before putting it in the hamper.

Now do you know why you don't have to plant mold seeds? Wherever there is food, air, and moisture, some mold spores will almost certainly settle and begin to grow.

The spore gets busy right away. It sprouts a few threads which it uses like soda straws to suck up food and water. After a short time it sends out runner threads. Each one of these becomes a new plant and sends out more runners. Perhaps you have seen strawberry plants growing. They spread in the same way.

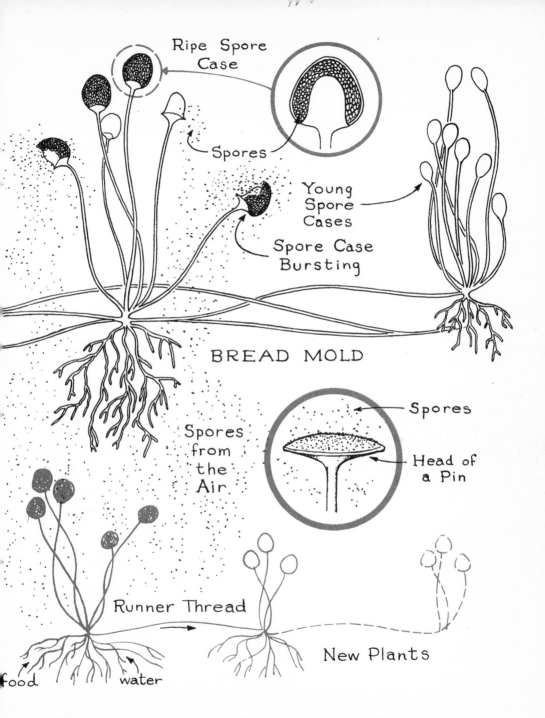

Ripe Spore Case

Spores

Young Spore Cases

Spore Case Bursting

BREAD MOLD

Spores from the Air

Spores

Head of a Pin

Runner Thread

New Plants

food   water

HOW MOLDS GROW AND SPREAD

Not all spores are carried in the air. There are some molds that grow in water and others that grow in the soil. The spores of these two kinds of mold have little thread-like tails which they use like outboard motors to move them around while they look for a growing-place. They are called *zoospores* (say: *ZO-o-spores*) because they can move themselves about like little animals. *Zoo* comes from the Greek word for animal.

If a spore doesn't find the food, air, and water it needs right away, it doesn't die. It just waits. It may remain alive for years in spite of heat, cold or drought. There are so many spores and they are so durable, that if there were plenty of food and water for them, molds might soon cover the entire earth!

There are always mold spores on the skins of fruit but as long as the fruit is dry the spores can't grow. However, if the skin is damaged and some of the juice leaks out, or if it has been lying on the wet ground, the spores quickly begin to sprout. Soon their threads penetrate the fruit and cause it to spoil.

This is why only hand-picked fruit is shipped over long distances. Just a few bruised, wet apples in a freight car can cause the whole shipment to arrive covered with mold!

Chapter III

THE SANITATION SQUAD

When autumn comes and leaves fall from the trees, do you ever use the rake to help tidy up the yard? Do you sometimes take out the garbage or empty the waste-paper baskets?

Wherever people live they clean house and take away trash. Did you ever wonder who does the housekeeping in the places where no one lives? Let's think about what would happen in the forests and fields if the cleaning were never done at all.

The leaves would pile up and up, year after year. So would the fallen branches and the dead trees. In a few hundred years the whole forest would be filled up. The trash would be higher than the trees had been. The grasses and the weeds and the flowers and all the birds and animals that died would pile up, too. The orchards would be stacked to the top with fallen fruit. The country lanes would disappear completely under great heaps of rubbish.

Do you know why this doesn't happen? It is mostly because of molds. Molds are nature's sanitation department.

Actually, the molds don't do all the work themselves. But they do a large part of it, and they make it possible for other microbes to help.

Molds do a very good clean-up job. The floors of our forests have not become piled up. The meadows are not choked with old grass that won't let new grass grow. Only very rarely do we come across a dead animal. This is amazing when you think of all the animals that must have died since the first animal was born. When plants and animals die, they just seem to disappear from the face of the earth after a while.

This is what happens to them: Let's picture an apple that has fallen from a tree. We already know that if the skin has been broken in the fall or if the ground is wet, molds will begin to grow. The molds spread rapidly as they feed on the sugar in the apple. This makes the apple soft and mushy.

Now the apple is good food for other kinds of microbes which could not have fed on it when it was hard. Before long, the apple isn't an apple anymore. It has been changed into water, into a gas called *carbon dioxide* which becomes part of the air, and into several minerals. The minerals dissolve and are washed into the earth as soon as it rains. Now there is nothing left of the apple to see at all. Even those seeds which have not sprouted are gone.

This is certainly a very good clean-up job—but it's much more than just a clean-up job. It is a job of such importance that if it were not done, everything and everybody on earth would die!

This is why: Green plants can't grow without minerals from the earth and carbon dioxide from the air. They take what they need to live just the way you take food from your pantry. But you know that you can't take

MEAT

PLANT FOODS

CARBON DIOXIDE GAS

MOLDS AND MICROBES ATTACK WASTE MATTER

MINERALS

food from the pantry forever without putting any into it. It has to be restocked once in a while. The same thing is true of minerals and carbon dioxide. If they were never restocked, they would soon be all used up.

If the plants had no food they would die. And if the animals had no plants to eat *they* would die. And if there were no plants or animals, what would *you* eat?

But thanks to the busy microbes, all the food that is taken from the earth and the air is returned. The microbes make a lending library of the earth's food. Everything is used for a while—then, just like a library book, it is returned and is ready for the next user. An animal eats grass. When the animal dies, molds and other microbes change it into gases and minerals for the soil. New grass grows in the fertilized soil. Another animal eats the grass and the same thing happens again. In this way, none of the food that plants and animals and people eat is ever used up. It is changed into many different forms but it can always be used again. It will last forever.

The next time you eat a potato or a lamb chop, think of this: Some little part of what you are eating may once have been part of a tiger or a caterpillar or an oak tree!

Chapter IV

MOLDS to EAT and DRINK

When we see mold on bread or fruit we say that the food is spoiled and we throw it away. We don't like to eat moldy food. The mold has changed the flavor. It does not taste good anymore.

But this is only true of foods that become moldy accidentally. Some foods are made moldy on purpose. The moldy flavor is exactly what people like about them. This is particularly true of certain cheeses.

All cheeses are milk products. *Camembert* (say: *KAM-em-bare*) cheese is made by mixing the spores of one of the Penicillium molds (this one is called, of course, *Penicillium camemberti*) into the milk. As the molds feed themselves on the milk they make certain changes in it. This change gives the cheese its delicious, tangy flavor.

Camembert cheese usually comes wrapped in foil. The first time we undo the wrapper, we are surprised. The cheese looks spoiled. The entire outside is covered with thick, gray-green mold. This is never trimmed off.

You eat it with the cheese. If you are a Camembert lover, you think the mold is the best part.

Roquefort (say: *ROKE-fert*) cheese goes a step further. There is no danger that anyone will trim off the mold. It runs all through the cheese like the veins in marble—or the chocolate in marble cake.

The cheese gets its name from the town of Roquefort, France. It has been made there for a long, long time. When the cheese makers are ready to start their work, they put some bread into damp caves. They leave it there until it gets moldy. Then they mix the moldy bread with the milk that is used to make the cheese.

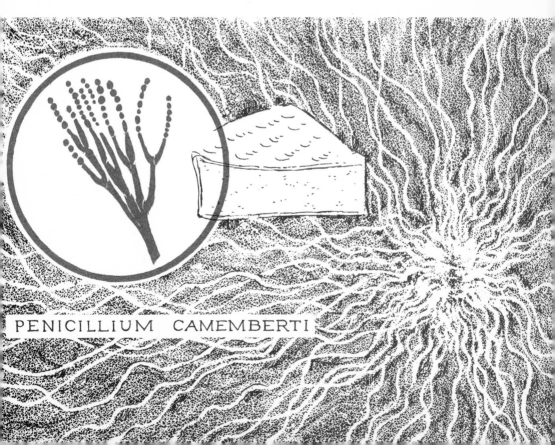

PENICILLIUM CAMEMBERTI

PENICILLIUM
ROQUEFORTI

The cheeses are formed into thick, round discs. The discs are called "wheels" because they are as large as wagon wheels. Molds can't grow without air. Since the molds can't get any air inside the big cheese wheels, they would soon die if the cheese makers didn't come to their rescue.

The cheese makers stick the cheese all over with big, long needles. This makes air-tunnels through the cheese. The molds grow in these tunnels. They fill them completely with the blue-green spores which give Roquefort cheese its special appearance and flavor.

Before about 1900, cheese makers were sometimes unpleasantly surprised when a strange mold grew in their cheese. They never knew how it would taste and sometimes it wasn't good at all. Nowadays, molds for cheese are specially grown. A cheese maker can go to a dairy supply firm and purchase exactly the kind of spores he wants instead of taking a chance.

There are also molds which give a special flavor to wine. They grow only in certain areas, particularly the Rhine valley and in parts of Hungary. The wines from these places are highly prized.

There is an interesting story about how one of these molds was discovered many centuries ago.

The Bishop of Mayence, in the Rhine valley of Germany, was in charge of enormous vineyards. Every year, as soon as the grapes began to ripen, the vineyards were closed. No one was permitted to enter until the bishop gave the signal for the grape harvest to begin.

But one year the bishop fell ill. The grapes ripened. It was time for the harvest. The peasants were ready but the poor bishop was silent. He was much too sick to think of grapes and wine.

The peasants grew sad as they saw the overripe grapes turn moldy. A gray powder spread over the grapes. Finally, they turned brown and began to dry up.

It wasn't until November that the bishop was well enough to give the signal for the harvest to begin. It did not seem worthwhile to gather those miserable looking grapes—still, the bishop had given the signal. The peasants obeyed. They picked the grapes.

Imagine everyone's surprise when the wine pressed from the moldy grapes turned out to be the best anyone had ever tasted!

Chapter V

MIRACLE MOLDS

More than three thousand years ago the Chinese used moldy soy beans to cure skin diseases. And the Indians of Central America used molds to cure infected wounds.

To these early people a cure was a kind of magic. They did not know why it worked. It just did. Only in modern times did men find out that the cure was not magic, but microbes.

It was *Louis Pasteur* (say: *LOO-ee Pas-TER*), a great French scientist born in 1822, who discovered that some diseases are caused by certain microbes—or germs, as they are more commonly called. Diseases caused by germs! This was one of the greatest discoveries of all time. But Pasteur did not stop his work with this discovery. He soon found out that some germs (or microbes) could kill other germs. Here was the beginning of a branch of modern medicine.

Pasteur died in 1895. But there were many others who carried on his work. They made a number of improvements in medicine—and then, in September, 1928, something really wonderful happened. A mold spore floated through an open window. . . .

Alexander Fleming was at work in his laboratory at Saint Mary's Hospital in London, England. It was a warm day and the windows were open. A dish of disease germs, needed for an experiment, had been left uncovered. It looked like cloudy soup. As Fleming walked by he glanced at the dish. Something caught his eye. He looked again. There was a patch of blue-green Penicillium mold growing on the dish. BUT—instead of cloudy soup, thick with germs, there was a clear circle all around the mold. All of the germs near the mold were dead!

Fleming knew that this was something important. He scraped off the bit of mold and put it in a dish of its own with some food. The mold plant spread and the blue-green patch grew larger. When it was big enough, Fleming set to work to find out why the mold had killed the germs. After many weeks of difficult experiments, he finally managed to squeeze from the mold a few drops of brownish fluid. This remarkable fluid was the germ-killer. Fleming named it *penicillin* (say: *pen-i-SILL-in*).

Penicillin turned out to be a far greater germ-killer than anything ever known before. But it took *so* long to make even a drop of it! Even though it was surely a valuable drug, Fleming decided that making penicillin was not practical. He went on with his other work.

PENICILLIUM
NOTATUM

SIR ALEXANDER FLEMING

Ten years later, in 1938, Dr. Florey and Dr. Chain, of Oxford University, read about Fleming's discovery. They were looking for a new medicine that would help people who were wounded in World War II. Penicillin seemed like the perfect answer. But when they tried to make it, they found the work very slow, just as Fleming had.

They had finally managed to make a few drops of penicillin when they heard about a London policeman who was dying in a hospital. He had a blood infection for which there was no cure. Florey and Chain began to give him penicillin. The policeman improved very quickly. He was almost well when the supply of penicil-

HAROLD W. FLOREY AND ERNEST B. CHAIN

lin ran out. It took so long to make more that the poor policeman got sick again and died.

But by now the scientists were sure they had a real miracle drug. It seemed to cure many diseases—among them, *pneumonia* (say: *new-MO-nia*), scarlet fever and *rheumatic* (say: *roo-MAT-ik*) fever. But England was at war. The whole country was busy fighting German bombs. There was no time for penicillin in England.

Finally, Dr. Florey and his fellow-workers decided to come to the United States which was not yet at war. They came in 1941. They promptly started a search for a better Penicillium mold.

They sent a helper out every morning to buy all the moldy fruit she could find in the market. People laughed at her. They called her "Moldy Mary." One morning "Moldy Mary" went to a fruit store. She came back with a very moldy cantaloupe. The mold on that cantaloupe was a different kind of Penicillium. It gave two hundred times as much penicillin as Fleming's original mold!

The drug companies soon found ways to make penicillin in large tanks. By 1946 there was enough to treat seven million patients a year. The age of miracle molds had come—but it had only just begun.

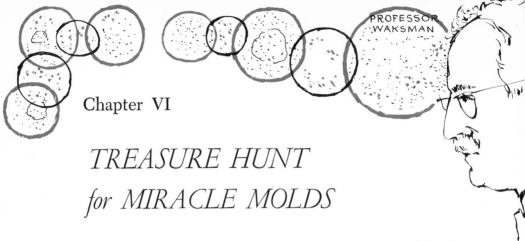

PROFESSOR WAKSMAN

Chapter VI

TREASURE HUNT
for MIRACLE MOLDS

Penicillin was discovered by a series of lucky accidents. There was an open window, a passing breeze, a floating spore, a dish of germ-broth, and an alert scientist.

No one expected a second miracle mold to come along in the same way. Scientists knew that they would have to search for it.

So the search began. In laboratories all over the United States teams of workers started to test all kinds of molds.

The first important discovery was made by Professor Waksman at Rutgers University. He tested ten thousand molds that grow in the soil. He tried each one in a germ dish like Fleming's. He kept looking hopefully for the clear ring around the mold. And one day, there it was. He called his new drug *streptomycin* (say: *strep-toe-MY-sin*).

Streptomycin worked against many diseases that were not cured by penicillin. Among these were typhoid (say: *TIE-foid*) fever and tuberculosis (say: *Tew-burr-*

kew-LOW-sis). But there were still many germs that were not killed by either drug. Scientists were sure that, hidden in the earth, were many, many more miracle molds. They had to be found—but how?

Then the American scientists had a wonderful idea. They decided to write letters to people who travelled to distant parts of the world. Perhaps there were valuable secrets in the soil of other countries. Perhaps the travellers could help to find them. Letters went out to air-line pilots, missionaries, explorers, salesmen, and even people on vacations. Each one was asked to send a package of earth from every place he visited.

The packages poured in from South America, Europe, Africa, and Asia. They came in astonishing numbers. Each one bore a label that told exactly where it had been found.

Every single sample of soil was tested. Every one was allowed to grow on a germ dish. And each time, the clear ring was watched for. There were many failures—but not all.

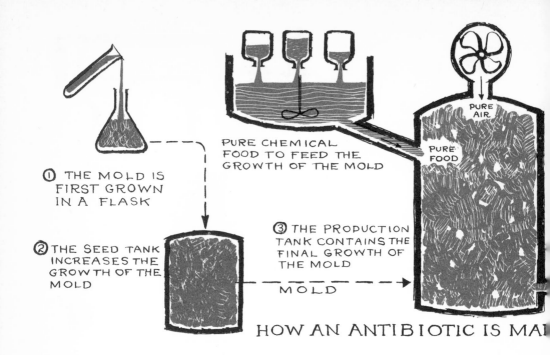

① THE MOLD IS FIRST GROWN IN A FLASK

② THE SEED TANK INCREASES THE GROWTH OF THE MOLD

PURE CHEMICAL FOOD TO FEED THE GROWTH OF THE MOLD

③ THE PRODUCTION TANK CONTAINS THE FINAL GROWTH OF THE MOLD

MOLD

PURE AIR

PURE FOOD

HOW AN ANTIBIOTIC IS MA[I]

During the years of the 1940's the laboratory workers tested more than a hundred thousand molds. They found *Aureomycin* (say: *or-ee-o-MY-sin*), *Chloromycetin* (say: *klor-o-my-SEE-tin*) and then *Terramycin* (say: *ter-uh-MY-sin*). Terramycin alone can cure one hundred diseases!

The engineers in the drug factories worked just as hard as the laboratory people. It wasn't easy to grow molds in the big batches needed. In shallow laboratory dishes, the molds got plenty of air. In the large tanks that the drug companies used, the molds did not get enough air, and they died.

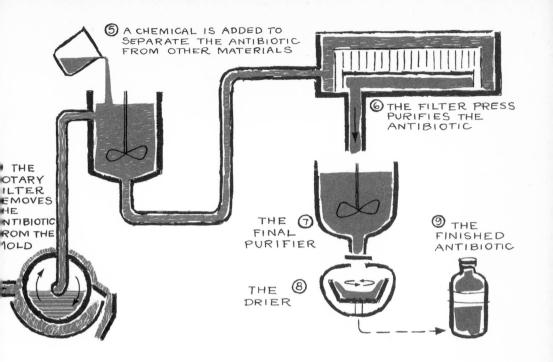

⑤ A CHEMICAL IS ADDED TO SEPARATE THE ANTIBIOTIC FROM OTHER MATERIALS

⑥ THE FILTER PRESS PURIFIES THE ANTIBIOTIC

⑥ THE ROTARY FILTER REMOVES THE ANTIBIOTIC FROM THE MOLD

THE ⑦ FINAL PURIFIER

⑨ THE FINISHED ANTIBIOTIC

THE ⑧ DRIER

The engineers decided to pump air through the tanks. But air might contain spores of other molds and spoil the medicine. And so the air had to be carefully purified first. And so did all the air in the factory. One drug company boasts that the cleanest air in the world is found, not on a mountain top, but in its own plant!

The work still goes on. Every day new molds are examined and new medicines are discovered. Dr. Waksman, the discoverer of *streptomycin*, worked with Dr. Lechevalier on *neomycin* (say: *nee-o-MY-sin*), another important drug. More recently, this same team found *candicidin* (say: *can-di-SIDE-in*). Candicidin is ex-

37

pected to cure many fungus diseases of both humans and plants.

There is a special name for all the miracle drugs made from molds. They are called *antibiotics* (say: *anty-by-OT-ics*). Antibiotic comes from the Latin word—*anti,* against, and the Greek word—*bios,* life. It means *against life.* It doesn't mean against *human* life, though. It means against germ life. Antibiotics are very much *for* human life. They save countless numbers of lives every year.

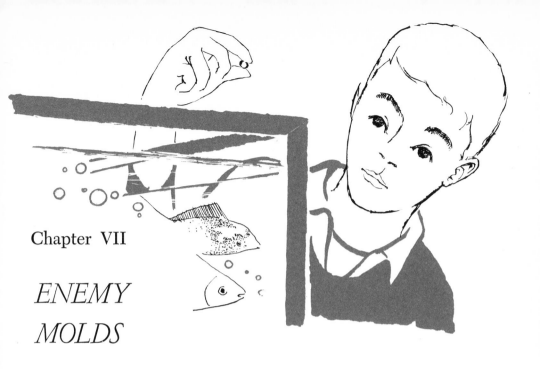

Chapter VII

ENEMY MOLDS

Most molds are our great friends. They do many useful jobs for us. But, unfortunately, mixed with the friends, there are a few enemies.

Most of the molds we have talked about so far live on dead things—cloth, bread, cheese. There are some molds that live on things that are alive. They are called *parasites* (say: *PAR-a-sites*).

These molds can be a great nuisance. There are some that get under human skin. They cause itchy skin ailments. Two of the most common harmful molds are called *ringworm* and *athlete's foot*.

Some molds attack live fish. We all know that fish eat plants. But when plants eat the fish—that's a serious matter. There are always water-borne mold spores in a pond or a fish tank. They cannot grow on a fish with healthy, unbroken skin. But just as an apple is open to molds as soon as it has a bruise, so is a fish.

If a fish scrapes against a rock, or gets a scratch or a bite in a fight with another fish, the waiting spore moves in. The mold grows quickly. The fish is soon covered with a thick, white fuzz. As the molds grow they feed on the fish. They actually eat the fish alive.

If you have a fish tank and see mold on a fish you can probably save the fish if you act very promptly. There are medicines that will kill the mold.

Farmers have a very serious problem with molds called *smuts* and *rusts*. The smuts look like sooty black spots. The rusts look just the way you think they do—rusty. They both ruin farm crops.

Wheat rust has probably been destroying wheat for as long as people have grown wheat. But we have only known for about a hundred years that it is a mold.

Several centuries ago farmers noticed that whenever there were barberry bushes near the wheat fields the wheat rust killed the crops. They didn't know why this happened but they found the right cure.

In 1755, the colony of Massachusetts passed a law called: "An act to prevent Damage to English Grains arising from Barberry Bushes." The farmers were given

ON
WHEAT
STALKS

ON
BARBERRY
BUSH LEAVES

WHEAT RUST

five years to destroy all their barberry bushes. After that time, they were fined two shillings for every barberry bush found on their land.

We know now that the wheat rust fungus grows in a strange way. It must spend part of its life on a barberry bush before it can move to the wheat. Even though the colonial farmers did not understand the life story of the rust, they made a good guess and passed a wise law.

Another farm enemy is the *potato blight,* a mildew type of mold. During the 1800's, potatoes were the chief crop of Ireland. Most of the Irish depended on them for food. Between 1845 and 1851 all of the potatoes were ruined by potato blight mildew.

POTATO BLIGHT

The Irish people did not have enough to eat and about a million of them died of starvation. Hundreds of thousands of others left Ireland and came to the United States. You probably have some friends whose ancestors came here from Ireland to escape the potato famine.

For years no one understood what caused the potato blight. Prizes were offered to anyone who could find the answer. There were many strange guesses. In one place, a new railroad had been built near the potato fields. As the locomotives went by, sparks flew from the rails. Some people thought that the sparks were caused by electricity, and that it was the electricity that killed the potatoes!

In 1885, Anton De Bary found that the blight was caused by a mold. As soon as this was known, people began to find ways to fight it. The best method was to burn all the diseased potatoes. In this way, the mold spores would not be carried to healthy potatoes.

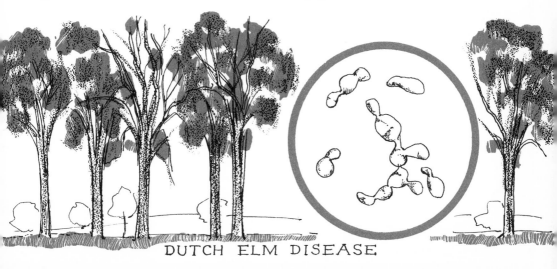

DUTCH ELM DISEASE

There are other molds which damage oats, corn, onions, apples, and white pine trees. However, modern chemistry has found ways to control most of them. Spraying the plants and treating the soil keep most crops free from enemy molds.

One of the few mold problems we have not yet solved is the Dutch elm disease. This fungus will kill all of our elm trees if a cure is not found for it soon.

Chapter VIII

YEAST— THE BAKER'S FRIEND

Have you ever made paste of flour and water? When it dries, it is hard and brittle. Bread is made of flour and water, too, but a slice of it is soft and fluffy. The reason bread is so different from paste is that it contains *yeast*. The yeast makes it light and soft instead of hard and crumbly.

Yeasts are really the first cousins of molds. Like molds they are microbes. Like molds they are fungi (food-robbers). They also serve us in many of the same ways as molds.

But they are not exactly the same. Many yeasts can live and grow without air; molds cannot. Most yeasts do not have spores. They grow by *budding*, instead.

YEAST CELLS GROW BY BUDDING

A yeast plant (or cell) has an oval shape. When it is ready to bud, a little bump begins to grow on one side. The bump (or bud) grows larger and larger. As soon as it is full size, it breaks away from the parent cell and starts life on its own. It takes only about thirty minutes for a yeast bud to become fully grown and start to make a brand new bud. Sometimes, instead of just one bud, three or four grow from one cell at the same time.

For as long as people have been writing history (about five thousand years) they have written of bread and wine. Both bread and wine are made by yeasts.

Loaves of bread have been found in Egyptian pyramids built six thousand years ago. Probably the ancient

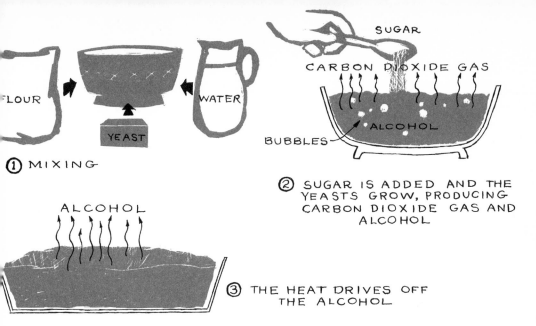

① MIXING

② SUGAR IS ADDED AND THE YEASTS GROW, PRODUCING CARBON DIOXIDE GAS AND ALCOHOL

③ THE HEAT DRIVES OFF THE ALCOHOL

HOW YEAST IS USED IN BREADMAKING

Egyptians didn't know that yeasts were plants. But they did find out that if they added yeast to their flour and water dough, it made the dough "rise." We still use yeast in exactly the same way when we make bread.

Yeasts feed on sugar. We add a little sugar to the flour and water and the yeasts begin to grow. As they grow, they change the sugar into two new chemicals—carbon dioxide gas and alcohol. The gas bubbles through the thick dough. It tries to find its way out. As it goes, it leaves little holes in the dough.

Did you ever blow through a soda straw and make a big froth of bubbles in your glass? If you blew hard enough, the liquid bubbled right up to the top of the glass—or maybe over the sides. Well, the yeasts blow gas through the dough in the same way. The bubbles stay behind and the dough becomes all puffy, like a sponge. When bread is baked in the oven, the heat drives off the alcohol that was formed. It evaporates into the air. None of it is left in the bread. The heat also kills the yeast plants so they do not continue to grow after the bread is baked.

Wine is also made when the yeasts feed on sugar and form carbon dioxide and alcohol. But in this case, it is the alcohol that is kept. Wine is not baked in an oven, like bread. The alcohol does not evaporate but remains in the fruit juice. The carbon dioxide gas, however,

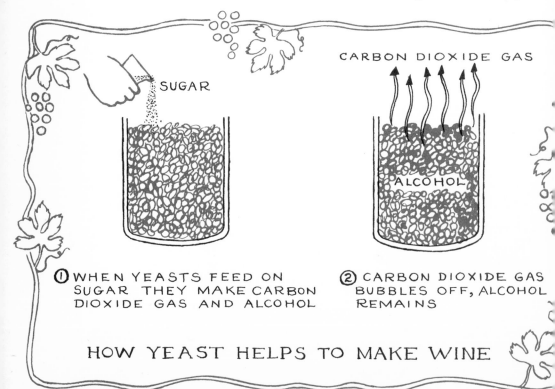

SUGAR

CARBON DIOXIDE GAS

ALCOHOL

① WHEN YEASTS FEED ON SUGAR THEY MAKE CARBON DIOXIDE GAS AND ALCOHOL

② CARBON DIOXIDE GAS BUBBLES OFF, ALCOHOL REMAINS

HOW YEAST HELPS TO MAKE WINE

easily bubbles away through the liquid and is lost into the air.

Nothing is needed to make wine except fruit and a container. There is sugar in the fruit and there are always yeasts on the skin of the fruit. Yeasts float around in the air just as mold spores do. They are also carried from grape to grape or berry to berry by birds and insects. A grape from the New York State wine district usually has between one thousand and three hundred thousand yeasts on it. If the grape has been pecked by a bird or bitten by a wasp it may bear as many as sixty million yeasts! Once a grape skin has been injured, the yeasts grow very fast. For this reason, the grapes are crushed to start the wine making. European peasants used to spread the grapes in large, shallow bowls and trample them with their bare feet!

Yeast also has many other uses. It is used to make beer and other beverages. And it is used in many factories for industrial purposes. Great quantities of it serve to change molasses or grain into alcohol.

The wine, beer, and alcohol industries are all important, but not nearly so important as bread making. Almost everybody in the United States eats bread every single day. Do you eat bread every day?

It takes a lot of gas bubbles to puff up a lump of heavy, sticky dough into nice light, spongy bread. When you think of how tiny yeasts are (sixty million of them can fit on a single grape!) it seems almost impossible that they can do such hard work. The next time you enjoy a slice of fresh bread, think of all the little yeast plants that helped the baker make it.

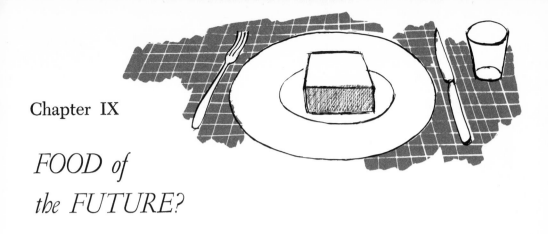

Chapter IX

FOOD of the FUTURE?

Nowadays, people live much longer than they did in times past. We know more about good health habits, we have better food, and we have miracle drugs to cure us when we are ill. Many more people are born now than die each year. The world is getting more and more people all the time.

Some scientists think that if this goes on for hundreds of years, the world will run out of food. There will be so many people that there won't be enough room left for the large ranches and farms it will take to feed them.

To solve this problem, we must find new kinds of food that can be grown in less space. There have been many good suggestions but the most interesting one is—you have probably guessed it—a diet based on molds and yeasts!

Yeast is a very good substitute for meat. It has almost the same food value. A kind of yeast has been discovered which tastes almost exactly like meat. It is cheap to grow. It grows very fast. If we start with five hundred pounds

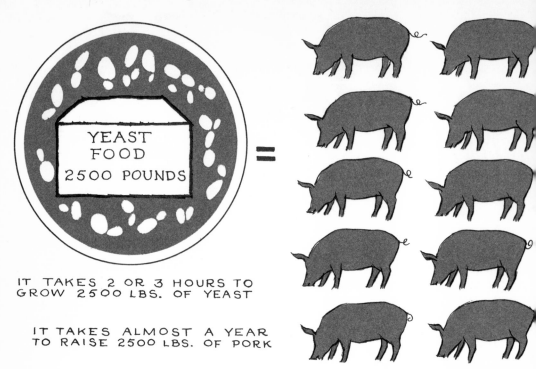

YEAST
FOOD
2500 POUNDS

=

IT TAKES 2 OR 3 HOURS TO
GROW 2500 LBS. OF YEAST

IT TAKES ALMOST A YEAR
TO RAISE 2500 LBS. OF PORK

of yeast in a tank we can have twenty-five hundred pounds in a couple of hours. To get the same amount of food in the form of pork, we would have to kill ten pigs —and it takes almost a whole year to raise a pig.

If necessary, we could get along without animals for food altogether. We could raise yeasts instead. It would be faster, cheaper, and much less work. But we would still need green plants. So far, we don't know of any way to make sugar or starch as fast or as cheap as plants can.

Molds are a good meat substitute, too, but not as good as yeasts. However, they seem to make an excellent chicken food.

A few years ago, an experiment was made at a poultry farm in the United States. Dried mold was ground up and mixed with corn. The people at the farm hoped that the chickens wouldn't know the difference and would eat the mold along with the corn. But the chickens *did* know the difference. They loved the mold. They picked out every little bit of it and only ate the corn when the mold was all gone!

Of course, it is not likely that people will dine on molds and yeasts for many, many years. But it does look as if farm animals may find them on the menu more and more often.

It isn't really a surprise that new ways to use molds and yeasts are still being discovered. Over the years we have found so many ways in which they help us: They flavor our food, they are nature's sanitation department, they make us well, they help us cook, they may one day feed us. As time goes by we will surely find many new jobs for our tiny servants.

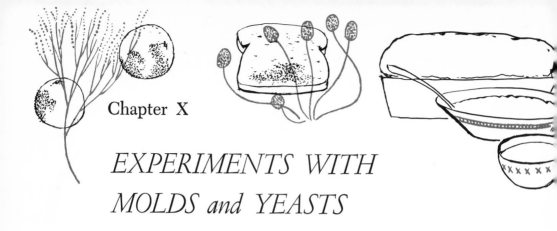

Chapter X

EXPERIMENTS WITH MOLDS and YEASTS

You have read a great deal about molds and yeasts. Now you are ready to be a scientist and do some experiments. You are ready to grow some mold of your own.

BREAD MOLDS

Take two slices of bread and break them in half. Wipe each piece across the floor or across a window sill. This will pick up some mold spores. Now dampen the bread by sprinkling some water from your fingertips. Be careful not to make the bread too wet or it will fall apart. Put each piece into a jar with a screw cover and close the cover. Put the jars away in a warm, dark place—a closet is fine. You have given the spores everything they need. They have food (the bread), water, and air that is trapped in the jar. They don't really need warmth, but it makes them grow more quickly.

After two or three days take out the jars and open them. What do you see on the bread? Some of the mold

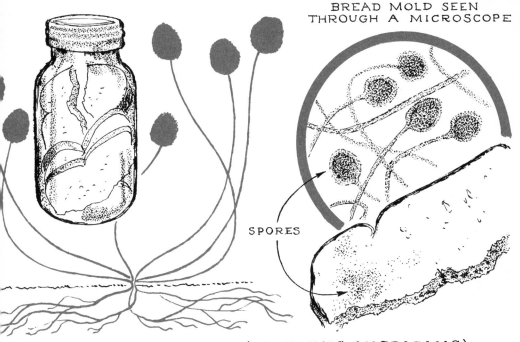

SPORES

GROWING BREAD MOLD (RHIZOPUS NIGRICANS)

will be a fluffy, white growth peppered with black spores on top. This is common bread mold. Its scientific name is *Rhizopus nigricans* (say: *RYE-zo-pus NIG-ri-cans*). Your experiment has been a success.

If you look carefully at the mold you will probably find some that is blue-green. This is Penicillium. Even though you may have grown some Penicillium on your bread, it usually grows best on fruit. Let's grow some for our next experiment.

Rub a knife blade through the blue-green mold on the bread. Now use the knife to make several deep cuts in the skin of an orange. If there was no Penicillium on your bread, make a few cuts in the orange and rub it on the floor. Put the orange into a covered jar with a piece of wet cotton in the bottom. This will keep it moist. Keep it in a warm, dark place for a week or ten days. When the orange is moldy, take it out of the jar and examine it carefully. Do you see tiny drops of amber colored liquid on the tips of the mold? It is from these small drops of moisture that penicillin is made!

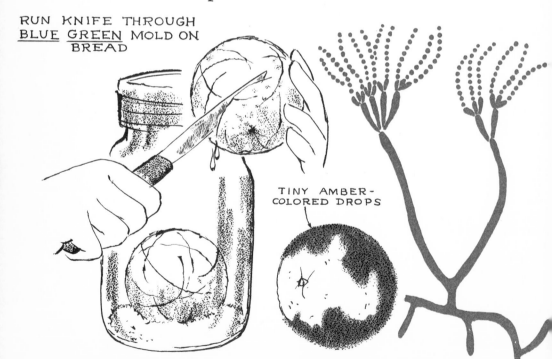

RUN KNIFE THROUGH
BLUE GREEN MOLD ON
BREAD

TINY AMBER-
COLORED DROPS

HOW TO GROW PENICILLIUM ON AN ORANGE

There are many yeast experiments but let's do the one that is the most fun. We'll bake bread. If you do it properly you will be able to eat the results of your experiment!

BREAD

You will need: 1 saucepan
1 large bowl
1 loaf pan
1 bread board
1 cup
1 package of yeast from the grocery store (either a cake or granulated)
1 cup of milk
3 cups of flour
1½ teaspoons of salt
1 tablespoon of sugar
1 tablespoon of butter
extra butter for greasing the pan and bowl

57

Put the milk in the saucepan and heat it until it begins to come up to the top of the pan. Remove it from the stove quickly, before it spills over the sides of the pan. Set it aside to cool. Wait until it is lukewarm. This means that a few drops sprinkled on the inside of your wrist do not feel hot, just slightly warm. Yeast plants are killed by too much heat, so be very careful about this.

When the milk is cool enough, put four tablespoons of it into a cup. Add the yeast and stir. If you have granulated yeast, just sprinkle it in. If it is a yeast cake, crumble it first. Put it aside for a few minutes to let the yeast dissolve. While you are waiting, put the rest of the milk into the large bowl. Add the butter, sugar and salt. When the yeast is soft, add it to the bowl. Stir in the flour.

The dough will be very hard to mix. You will have to knead it instead. Rub a little flour on the bread board and turn out all the dough from the bowl onto the board. To knead, you press hard on the dough with your hands

while you turn and mix it. At first, big globs of dough will stick to your fingers, but as you knead, the dough will get smoother and won't stick as much. When the dough doesn't stick to the board anymore and is full of bubbles, stop.

Rub some butter around the sides of the bowl you used before. You don't have to wash it first. Put the dough back in the bowl and cover it with a clean towel or napkin. Put it in a warm place and leave it for about one hour.

During this time, the yeast plants are very busy. They begin to grow and they bud into thousands and thousands of new plants. All the time they send streams of carbon dioxide bubbles through your dough.

At the end of an hour, the dough should be twice as high in the bowl as it was when you started.

Put it back on the board and knead it again for a minute or two. Now grease the loaf pan, shape the dough into a loaf and put it into the pan. Cover it and leave it

BAKING

in a warm place to rise as you did before. When the loaf is twice as high as the one you made, it is time to bake it.

Heat the oven to 350° first and bake the bread for about forty-five minutes. When it begins to shrink away from the sides of the pan, it is ready. Doesn't it smell delicious? And how does it taste? It's a good thing that all experiments are not as good to eat as this one. If they were, every single scientist would be too fat!

INDEX